Original title:
The Intimate Poetic Diary

Author: Paulina Pähkel
Editor: Jessica Elisabeth Luik
ISBN 978-9916-39-466-3

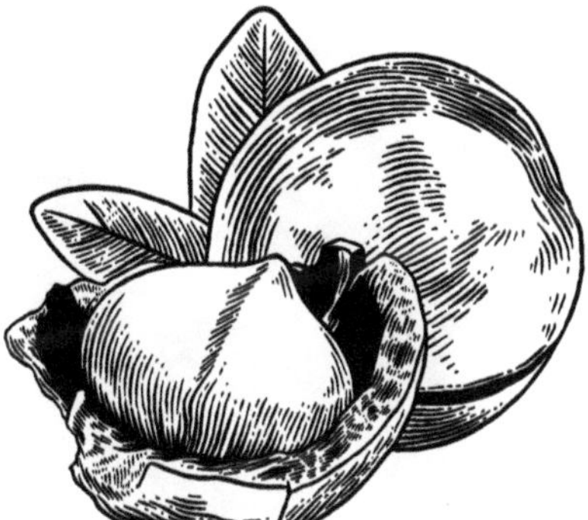

The Intimate Poetic Diary

Paulina Pähkel

Unseen Blossoms

In gardens veiled from eager eyes,
Where secret petals yearn for skies,
The timid buds in silence bloom,
Unseen, they give off sweet perfume.

Beneath the moon's soft, silver touch,
In night's embrace, they flourish much.
While all the world's asleep, they dance,
In unseen meadows, taking chance.

Their colors, vivid in the mind,
A tapestry of dreams entwined.
Though never graced by light of day,
In hidden glory they'll forever stay.

Whims of Whispers

In twilight's gleam where shadows play,
Whispers weave through willows grey.
Gently floating on the breeze,
Carrying secrets through the trees.

They rustle leaves with gentle might,
Dancing nimbly through the night.
Murmuring tales of ancient times,
Of lovers' passion, poets' rhymes.

Each soft sigh, a veiled intent,
Where quiet words are softly sent.
In every hush, a story lives,
To each listener, it cautiously gives.

Intimate Illusions

We clasp to shadows in our minds,
Illusions that our hearts unbind.
In intangible realms, we meet,
Where whispered souls and silence greet.

A tender gaze that no one sees,
A touch that's felt on a soft breeze.
Time's fabric warps, reality skews,
In the space where the unreal turns true.

When eyes close, the visions clear,
Intimate dreams draw ever near.
In that place, we hold what's lost,
Illusions warm as frost is to frost.

Glossary of the Guarded

With every word withheld, restrained,
The guarded heart's own lexicon explained.
Each silence speaks volumes untold,
In a book of thoughts kept closely hold.

Behind the shield of stoic guise,
The lexicon grows, compiles, lies.
In guarded whispers and cautious breath,
The language thrives on what's not said.

A dictionary of mute discourse,
Where quiet notions take their course.
The entries scribed in secret ink,
A glossary only the guarded think.

Subtextual Symphony

Beneath the veil of spoken words,
A deeper chord begins to play.
The heart in silent rhythm heard,
In subtextual ballet.

A glance, a sigh, the unspoken thought,
Compose the music's covert script.
Where feelings dance and never caught,
In secrecy adeptly slipped.

A mute concerto, softly spun,
From looks and whispers underneath.
The conversation now begun,
In symphony without a wreath.

Invisible notes in the air entwine,
A language that the soul deciphers.
In every pause, a hidden sign,
A symphony of silent lifers.

Enigmatic Entwining

In cryptic patterns, souls caress,
Embraced in enigmatic thread.
Tangled paths of tenderness,
Where silent sentiments are spread.

A labyrinth of linked fates,
Subtle and profound combine.
Two spirits in dance, that fate creates,
In enigmatic entwining they align.

Mysteries cloaked in each embrace,
Understanding deeper than the sea.
Eyes locked in a silent chase,
Where words are needless, hearts roam free.

Through the enigma, connections weave,
With every twist, a story told.
Entwined in ways we scarce believe,
In patterns far too vast to hold.

Quietudes of Quest

In the still of searching souls,
Whispers of yearning softly tread.
Across the silence, the bell tolls,
Marking paths where dreamers led.

Beneath the hush of twilight's gaze,
Journeys ventured in the calm.
Seeking out the dawn's first rays,
In quietude's unwavering balm.

Through forests of the unspoken word,
Trails of the tranquil quest unwind.
In the solitude, their hopes are heard,
In the sacred spaces of the mind.

Questers in the quiet find,
The truths that louder hours conceal.
In contemplation's deep-sea minds,
The quietudes of quest reveal.

Whispers of the Heart

In twilight's hush, my heart does speak,
Of love's soft touch, it's yours I seek.
The beating rhythm, a whispered tune,
Like gentle winds on dunes of June.

Beneath the moon's delicate glow,
My heart's secrets, I bestow.
In tender waves, the whispers start,
To paint the canvas of the heart.

Echos in the chamber, true and deep,
Where all my hopes and dreams do sleep.
In quiet beats, they stir, take part,
Within the whispers of the heart.

Sonnets of Silence

The silent sonnets play at dusk,
In every shadow, a twilight musk.
Words unsaid twirl in the air,
Scribing sonnets of silent prayer.

A ballet of moments, still and deep,
They pirouette while the world does sleep.
In the absence of sound, they rise and dance,
As moonlight through the silence glances.

A hush descends, the world at peace,
As silent sonnets find their release.
Whispered in the void, where echoes rest,
In the tranquility of silence, we're blessed.

Inward Blossoms

Seeds of potential lie in wait,
Beyond the hustle, stress, and hate.
In silence, thoughts begin to bubble,
Inward blossoms, free from trouble.

Nurtured by the soul's own light,
They bloom within, out of sight.
Blossoms of hope and inner fire,
Growing quietly, ever higher.

With every breath, roots reach deep,
Stirring from their tranquil sleep.
Each petal a story, a silent song,
Inward blossoms, where they belong.

Quiet Echoes of Passion

In the stillness, passions roar,
Softly as waves upon the shore.
Quiet echoes that resonate,
In the chamber where desires wait.

Unheard, yet felt in the soul's deep well,
Where dreams and yearnings swell.
A tender touch, a glance, a sigh,
In quiet echoes, passions fly.

Through silent nights, they gently creep,
In waking thoughts and in dreamful sleep.
The heart's silent drum in love's sweet ration,
Beats in the quiet echoes of passion.

Mosaic of the Mute

In silence lay a myriad piece
A tapestry where voices cease
Each fragment tells a tale unsaid
A symphony of thoughts unshed

Within this quiet, colors scream
A mute parade, a whispered dream
The void itself speaks volumes clear
In every gap, a story dear

A patchwork quilt of hush profound
Where secrets nestle, tightly wound
The silent echos form a bond
A speechless mosaic drawn beyond

Each shard and sliver finds its place
In this mute gallery of grace
A hallowed hush that all can hear
A mute mosaic held so dear

Passages of Privacy

Behind the doors of solitude
In corridors of quietude
Walls whisper with the breath of time
Guarding moments, yours and mine

Through the passages of privacy
Weave tales of hidden legacy
Alone with thoughts that softly tread
On floors of dreams too swiftly shed

Shadows stretch with secrets sown
In vaults of silence, seeds have grown
The heart's discourse without a voice
In privacy, we make our choice

Here, the self can softly bloom
Far from the relentless boom
Our cloistered whispers gently sway
In sacred passages, tucked away

Harmonies of Hesitation

The notes that quiver in the air
The pregnant pause of silent prayer
Tuning forks for souls alight
In the shallow breath of the night

Harmonies of hesitation
Sing of timid trepidation
Melodies of mute suspense
Suspended in the time immense

Every hesitant refrain
Carries echoes of a chain
That binds the potent, still unsung
In the chorus of the tongue

Within the rests, the music waits
Anticipating fates
The symphony of the unsure
Conducts the harmonies demure

Unadorned Artistry

Bare canvas whispers to the soul
A pristine tale yet to unroll
In every stroke, a pure intent
An artless truth that won't relent

The beauty in simplicity
Outshines the gaudy tapestry
Nature's hand, the greatest muse
Crafting hues that candidly infuse

Raw expression, unembellished
Truths that shine, unvarnished, relished
In the plain, the profound seeps
Where unadorned artistry sleeps

Unpretentious, clear and bright
The plain transformed into sight
An opus born from nothing more
Than authentic core

Brushstrokes of the Mind

In the canvas of thought, shades dance,
With every sweep, a vivid trance.
The bristles sway in tender mind's embrace,
Sketching dreams, leaving reality's trace.

With each hue, memories align,
In warp and weft, past and present entwine.
Silent whispers of color's bold decree,
Across the mind's expanse, a boundless sea.

A masterpiece of inner lore,
Escaping through the heart's pore.
Invisible to the world, it hides,
Within the soul, where truth abides.

Private Prelude

In quiet corners of the heart’s concave,
Where whispers build a secret enclave.
A prelude plays, soft and discrete,
An overture for emotions to meet.

A symphony of silent yearning,
In the chamber of solitude, burning.
This prelude, private, serene,
Composes melodies, unheard, unseen.

Strings of the soul, gently pluck,
In the hushed hall, no need for luck.
A private prelude, a silent plea,
In love's own language, free yet flea.

Hues of Solitude

Solitude wraps its hues around me,
In layers of quietude, it found me.
A spectrum of thoughts, softly tread,
In the silence, where words fear to wed.

Painted in strokes of solace's art,
Each hue a beat from a lone heart.
In this gallery of peace, I stroll,
A collage of contemplation, filling my soul.

Crimson streaks of passion's play,
Muted blues where calm waters sway.
Alone, yet in colors, I confide,
Where solitude's hues gently abide.

Muted Metaphors

Words unspoken, metaphors muted,
In the silence, eloquence rooted.
Calmly they lie in hidden depth,
Breathing softly, in quiet breath.

In the mind's eye, they glow, yet restrained,
Untouched by the world, unsullied, unfeigned.
A tapestry woven with threads of thought,
In the loom of silence, metaphors caught.

They whisper in echoes of the unsaid,
Dancing in shadows that light has shed.
Metaphors, muted, but meaning scores,
Softly they speak, behind closed doors.

Labyrinth of Longing

In this maze of yearn and turns,
We search for light that softly burns.
With each wrong step, hope dwindles small,
Yet in our hearts, love's echo calls.

Walls of longing close and tight,
Hold whispered dreams far from sight.
Through winding paths and silent pleas,
We chase the warmth of memories.

Endless corridors of thought,
With tangled feelings, tightly wrought.
In the labyrinth of our desire,
We seek the flame that fuels the fire.

Shaded Haikus

Beneath the willow,
Leaves casting cool, dappled shade,
Whispers dance in breeze.

Sunset's soft farewell,
Pinks and oranges in play,
Day meets night's embrace.

Mountains tall and proud,
Silhouettes against the sky,
Guard time's endless march.

River's gentle flow,
Carving earth with liquid grace,
Stories shaped in stone.

Soft Shadows of Truth

Soft shadows of truth subtly lie,
Beneath the veils of alibis.
Half-lit secrets begin to stir,
Silence speaks what words defer.

In the dim light of the crescent moon,
Doubt whispers to the heart so soon.
Yet oft' the darkness makes us true,
Revealing what the day won't do.

Through the hushed and gentle gloam,
Honesty finds its way home.
In these shades, no need to prove,
Only to accept and move.

Cupped Confessions

In the quiet of our clasped hands,
Unsaid words find their demands.
The warmth between each finger's space,
Holds stories told without a trace.

Eyes avow with silent speech,
Tales the lips dare not to preach.
In breath-hushed moments do we share,
Cupped confessions, raw and bare.

Every crease and every line,
A testament of time's design.
In this hold, we find release,
A grip that grants us quiet peace.

Taboo Tapestry

In twilight's fold where secrets dwell,
Through whispered threads, a story swell.
The fabric of forbidden speech,
Weaves a truth we dare not preach.

In shadowed hues of scarlet sin,
The fibres twist, betwixt within.
Each stitch a pact of silent cries,
A patterned bond of hidden ties.

This tapestry of tacit lore,
With every knot, it guards the core.
Enigmatic, veiled allure,
Its taboo tales remain obscure.

In the forbidden weave we find,
The muted echoes of mankind.
A canvas wrought from fears and lies,
An artful shroud of thin disguise.

Murals from the Mind's Eye

Upon the walls of thought's enclave,
The mind's eye paints the scenes so brave.
A spectrum spills of dreams unsaid,
Where color's voice in quiet is shed.

Imagined tales come into light,
A mural grown from inner sight.
Each stroke endowed with silent might,
Commands the wall to banish night.

The artist's soul in pure display,
As myths and musings interplay.
In every hue, a whispered word,
A visual symphony unheard.

What minds conceive, they can create,
Upon the wall, they narrate fate.
In rapid strokes of genius strive,
Murals live, their scenes alive.

Confessional Canvases

Each painted scene a whispered sin,
Admissions brushed in hues begin.
The canvas soaks up every vice,
A priest to every heart's device.

In strokes of guilt, the layers build,
The bristles carry burdens, filled.
The palette blends the soul's remorse,
An artful, silent, sacred force.

Confessions dance in colors bold,
The silent whispers now unfold.
Each line releases stored unease,
Portraits of apology, they please.

A gallery of sins confessed,
On canvas lies the heart undressed.
Through every smear, a truth is known,
Reprieve in every color shown.

Diurnal Dreams

With dawn, the dreams of night take flight,
And in their place, the day's clear light.
Still, whispers of the dark remain,
In waking thoughts, they stake their claim.

A diurnal dream's soft hand does steer,
Through hours awake, yet still so near.
The dreamscape shifts to daytime's realm,
Beneath the sun, a subtle helm.

In each ambition, spark, and drive,
Nocturnal dreams are kept alive.
From visions' spring to action's stream,
Daylight bears the sleeper's dream.

When twilight blends to morning's gleam,
Reality inherits dream.
In every goal and choice we make,
Our nightly dreams the daylight take.

Inked Whispers

Upon the parchment, whispers glide,
In loops and lines where secrets hide.
Ink-dipped quill, a silent speaker,
Crafting words, the dreamer's seeker.

Muted utterances flow and merge,
The pen's ballet, a graceful surge.
Spiraled letters clutch the night;
Mysteries wrapped in silent flight.

Tales of love and shrouded sorrow,
Imprint today, erase tomorrow.
Each stroke inscribes a silent plea,
A tale untold, yet meant to be.

Whispers etched in midnight hue,
They live, they breathe, they speak to you.
Behind each whisper, truth unfurls,
Ink-sketched dreams, a canvas swirls.

Velvet Thoughts

In the fabric of the mind,
Velvet thoughts are soft, entwined.
Touching gently, whispers sweet,
Where heart's desires and musings meet.

Silken threads of conscious stream,
Draped in velvet, a subconscious dream.
Each thought a petal, smoothly laid,
In this mental tapestry, our feelings fade.

Subdued in touch, yet rich in hue,
Thoughts dance in depths, in shades anew.
Like velvet folds, they overlap,
Enveloping warmth, in comfort's wrap.

In dusky silence, smooth as night,
Ideas cloaked in soft twilight.
Velvety visions, gently brought,
In tender fabric, our dreams are wrought.

Pulse of the Unspoken

Beneath the hush, a heartbeat sounds,
In silent beats, it knows no bounds.
The pulse of words we dare not speak,
In rhythm known to soul's mystique.

It thrums in sync with quietude,
A symphony, in silent feud.
Tales unfold in hearts so deep,
In unvoiced thoughts, they stir, they creep.

The timbre of an inner tide,
In silence, secrets often hide.
Yet every unspoken truth resounds,
The pulse it beats, it leaps, it pounds.

Unuttered dreams, in silence, swell,
Their echoes paint where longings dwell.
The wordless stories' pulsing drone,
A language felt, heard, but unknown.

Woven Dreams

In the loom of night, dreams interlace,
A dance of threads in midnight space.
Woven tightly, hues of thought,
In intricate patterns, tenderly caught.

Stitched with the visions of slumber's hand,
Wrapped in the yarns of a far-off land.
Each strand a tale, spun soft and clear,
Weaving the fabric of dreams so dear.

Threads of hope intertwine with fear,
In this patchwork quilt, emotions peer.
With every weft and each warp's guide,
Narratives merge, and fates collide.

And when dawn's light begins to stream,
We hold the remnants of woven dream.
In the daybreak's gentle seams,
Lie the tattered edges of our night's weaves.

Tapestries of Thought

In the loom of mind, threads twist and twine,
Unseen hands weave the whispers of the mute,
Colors of dreams and memories combine,
Crafting a cloth where past and future suit.

Ideas dance in intricate array,
Patterns of passion and knowledge entwined,
Every emotion on display,
In the fabric of thoughts, our fates are lined.

Silken strands of consciousness intertwine,
With each thread, a narrative is spun,
In the tapestries, truths and myths align,
Under the watchful eye of the setting sun.

Philosophy's silver meets Science's gold,
In our minds, the greatest stories are told.

Secret Sonnets

Whispered words on a parchment pale,
Secret sonnets sail the silent sea,
Love's hidden tales, set adrift to hail,
The hearts that seek what could never be.

Lines laden with the weight of hidden truth,
A language lost to all but love's own ear,
In every verse, the vigor of youth,
In every rhyme, the trace of a tear.

Unspoken dreams in metaphor's tight embrace,
Longing locked in iambic feet,
Each sonnet a clandestine meeting place,
For souls that in shadows entreat.

Behind sealed lips, passions burn and flow,
In secret sonnets, love dares to speak low.

Flickers of Sentiment

A fleeting smile, the spark of connection's fire,
In smoldering glances, emotions conspire,
Each spark ignites a narrative's wick,
Stories in the flames, dancing quick.

Flickering hopes in the wind's soft sighs,
Candles of comfort in love's gentle eyes,
Fleeting feelings, brushed with tender care,
In the warmth of a moment willingly shared.

The glow of memory, a subtle flare,
That lights up the corners of hearts laid bare,
Each flicker, a verse in the heart's sweet song,
In the chamber of whispers, where sentiments belong.

Embers of yearning, a slow, soft burn,
In the dance of the flickers, we live and learn.

Hushed Heartbeats

In the stillness, hushed heartbeats resound,
Quiet cadences of love that's bound,
Softly drumming in a rhythmic thrall,
The sound of two hearts, synced in silent call.

Whispering blood, a muted drumming,
In the body's depths, ardently strumming,
Syncopated pulses, in tender time,
Compose a wordless poem, intimate and sublime.

Between breaths, a quiet pulse prevails,
A soft murmur when all else fails,
Soothing the spirit with its gentle beat,
In the hush, two lovers' hearts entreat.

Beneath the noise, beneath the din,
Hushed heartbeats speak of love within.

Intimacy en Vers

Whispered words in twilit rooms,
With gentle touch, the closeness blooms.
Eyes that speak when lips are near,
In every breath, love's cadence clear.

Two hearts in silent conversation,
Amidst the quiet, a foundation.
Fingers laced like woven thread,
In every pause, unspoken said.

Embrace that shelters from the storm,
In shared warmth, we find our form.
Breath to breath and beat to beat,
In every glance, our souls greet.

Words unneeded when souls entwine,
The simple act of hands in line.
In the dance of close-held sway,
Our spirits speak, love's ballet.

Subdued Echoes

In halls of memory, echoes faint,
A whispering past, a canvas quaint.
Shadows flit on musty walls,
Where history's soft footprint falls.

Timeworn tales and murmurs low,
Subdued echoes from long ago.
They linger in the aged air,
Ghosts of moments we once shared.

Silent are the voices past,
Yet in the mind, they holdfast.
Memories that time has cast,
Resound within, forever vast.

Bygone whispers, soft and hushed,
In the quiet, time is brushed.
Echoes in the heart's deep chambers,
Living on as quiet embers.

Quill and Quiver

With quill in hand, the poet's quiver,
Filled with thoughts that shake and shiver.
Words that flow like streams unchecked,
Crafting worlds from dreams elect.

Ink drops splatter, bold and free,
Telling tales that yearn to be.
On parchment plains, the dance begins,
With every line, the story spins.

Mighty quill, a simple spear,
Fights the silence all revere.
In strokes of genius, lines are born,
From the mind's eye, they are torn.

Spilling secrets, none can censor,
Through the quill, the soul's dispenser.
Canvas filled, the journey's over,
The quill rests; the page its lover.

Cloistered Stanzas

In cloistered halls of my own mind,
Stanzas sit, in silence twined.
Each line a breath of captured thought,
In knots of wisdom, tightly wrought.

Words like monks in quiet prayer,
Line by line, they build a lair.
Where meaning dwells and peace can stand,
In this inner, sacred land.

Verses veiled from world's profane,
Here contemplation's vineyards reign.
In the scriptorium of my heart,
Poetic rites, a sacred art.

Separated from day's clamor,
Here, my spirit dons its armor.
In cloistered verses, truth is gleaned,
In the script, my soul is cleaned.

Symphonies of Subtlety

In tender tones the twilight sings,
Its symphonies of subtlety,
A hush of wings, the evening brings,
A canvas vast for dreamers free.

With whispers soft the night will weave,
Its silver threads through sable sky,
In every starlit note, believe,
The universe will softly sigh.

A gentle breeze through leaves it flirts,
The murmurs form a silent score,
Each rustle like a violin skirts,
Around the heart to softly pour.

The moon above, a silent maestro,
Conducts the nocturne's tender flow,
Each shadow plays its part, its lustro,
In symphonies of subtlety, aglow.

Sanctuary of Syllables

Within the written word, find peace,
A sanctuary of syllables to lease,
Each letter laid with loving care,
Crafting solace from the air.

Upon the page, a world to hold,
A tale of whispers, inked and bold,
Words that wrap around the soul,
In gentle waves that make us whole.

Escape to where the verses bloom,
A silent room beyond the gloom,
A refuge from the noisy day,
Where syllables can dance and sway.

Here letters form a sacred space,
A haven from life's hectic pace,
In this abode of written grace,
Find solace in the text's embrace.

Reverent Rhymes

Beneath the ancient starlit dome,
Reside the verses of our home,
In reverent rhymes, they softly tread,
Upon the paths where thoughts are led.

Each line a prayer, each word a psalm,
In the quietude, a healing balm,
Through metered breath and tempo'd sounds,
Sanctity in verse abounds.

The cadence calls, a hymnal voice,
Invites the weary to rejoice,
In rhymes that echo through the night,
A sacred dance of worded light.

Within this temple made of prose,
A congregation of repose,
Gathers close in rhyme's sweet rooms,
To find their peace, where reverence blooms.

Inflorescence of the Id

Deep within the mind's own garden blooms,
An inflorescence of the Id's perfumes,
In colors vibrant, untamed desires,
Sprout from the soul's unconscious fires.

Thoughts like petals, wild and fierce,
In the psyche's soil, they pierce,
Stretching upwards, seeking light,
In the inner darkness, fight.

Freudian flowers, dreams unfurled,
In the cryptic, inner world,
Where each emotion, wish, and whim,
Through the stem of self does swim.

Thus the mind's own flora spread,
In the layered beds, they wed,
Casting shadows, casting seeds,
In the inflorescence of the Id's needs.

Chronicles of a Silent Love

In whispers of the quivering leaves,
Under the hush of starry skies,
A tale untold, quietly weaves,
Between the heartbeats and the sighs.

Shy glances shared, ne'er crossing paths,
Words unspoken, but eyes converse,
A secret bond that the heart crafts,
In the chronicles of the universe.

Moonlit dances with shadows cast,
Feelings hidden beneath the cloak of night,
Hoping this silent love might last,
Held in a gaze that feels so right.

Time inches on, yet feelings stay,
Painted in silence, love endures,
A quiet ballet of give and sway,
The chronicle silent, pure and sure.

Fabric of My Solitary Soul

Weaving threads of thoughts alone,
Silk strands of solitude entwined,
In the fabric of my soul, I've sown,
Patterns of peace that calms my mind.

Wrapped in layers of quietude,
The tapestry tells my silent tale,
In every knot, there's fortitude,
In every color, a dream that's pale.

Alone, but not in loneliness,
In my solitary soul's embrace,
Finding comfort in the stillness,
The fabric holds my solitary grace.

Let the world spin fast and wild,
In my realm, time gently flows,
Here lies the spirit, meek and mild,
The fabric of my soul in repose.

Dreams Stitched in Metaphor

Slumber's loom weaves a tapestry,
Threads of dreams through a needle's eye,
Stitched in metaphor, soft and free,
In the quiet quilt of a midnight sky.

Fantasies spun in silken yarn,
Castles and dragons in misty air,
A sailor's quest, a love to yearn,
Stitched in the sleep of a moonlit lair.

On the fabric of the night's imagination,
With each stitch, a story comes alive,
In the weave, there's gentle liberation,
Dreams stitched in metaphor thrive.

As dawn unravels the nightly seam,
Metaphorical threads in the daylight fade,
But in the heart remains the dream,
The magic of the night's embroidered parade.

Memories Etched in Rhyme

The past is a poem, each memory a verse,
Etched in the rhythm of rhyme,
A dance of words, for better or worse,
A melody played in the chime.

Those days of joy, now verses bright,
Scribed in the colors of our prime,
And even in sorrow's dimmest light,
There's comfort found in the rhyme.

In lines we remember the laughter shared,
The touch of love, the warmth divine,
In cadenced beat, nothing compared,
To memories in our hearts enshrined.

So read the stanzas, feel once more,
The echoes of time in poetic climb,
For life's a poem at its core,
Our memories etched in rhyme.

Scribed in Silence

In a world uproarious, loud and violent,
A soul writes in whispers, calm and silent.
Words fall like feathers upon the page,
In the still of night, the mind's own stage.

The chaos of day held at arm's length,
Silence is a fortress, solitude its strength.
Each stroke a secret, safely confined,
In the quietude, peace of mind is defined.

Phrases dance away from the turmoil,
Scribed in silence, safe from the spoil.
In the hush, the heart dares to speak,
Emotions painted strong, yet technique sleek.

Tranquility's pen moves with grace,
Transcribing whispers that time will not erase.
Pure and potent as a silent vow,
The words resonate, here and now.

Innermost Ink

With a pen dipped in the well of the soul,
The writer finds the script that makes them whole.
Stories untold, now vividly splay,
Innermost ink smeared across the fray.

Emotions surge, a tumultuous tide,
Scrawled onto paper, no need to hide.
Each line a pulse, each word a breath,
A symphony scribed, far from death.

Deep within the crevices, the truths spill,
Penning down dreams, aspirations to fulfill.
Tales of triumph, sagas of despair,
In the ink, the soul lays itself bare.

The quill's dance, an intimate link,
Capturing essence in innermost ink.
Artistry born from the depths within,
The transcript of being, skin to skin.

Reflections of Reverie

In the mirror of the mind's quiet lake,
Reflections of reverie begin to take shape.
Daydreams skim the surface, light and free,
Cascading thoughts, a flowing reverie.

Beneath the calm waters, visions bloom,
Where ideas and fantasies silently loom.
Ripples of longing, waves of bliss,
In reflection, find life's tender kiss.

Moments savored, sweet and soft,
In these reflections, aloft.
Times remembered, futures unseen,
Mingling in the middle, a tranquil dream.

The mind reflects, a well so deep,
Where reveries stir and memories seep.
In reflections cast by the heart's decree,
Lies the quiet beauty of reverie.

Heartstrings Unstrung

Once melodies played on heartstrings so tight,
Now echo the tunes of silence each night.
Where whispers of ardor once fervently clung,
Lie the remnants of heartstrings, raggedly unstrung.

In the hollow symphony of a love gone by,
The notes fall hollow, no tears left to cry.
Each pang a reminder of rhythms unsung,
The ballad of heartstrings, painfully unstrung.

Yet in dissonance, a new chord may arise,
The beauty in healing, the truth that defies.
From the discordant threads, new music is flung,
Restringing slowly the heartstrings once unstrung.

So let the heart beat to a tune that's new,
Finding strength in a melody true.
For even when old refrains have been wrung,
Love can restring the heartstrings unstrung.

Bared Beliefs

In silent contemplation, truths are sown,
A belief laid bare, in solitude grown.
Upon the canvas of the mind, it's etched,
A creed in stark relief, earnestly sketched.

Whispers of wisdom in the dead of night,
Ideas that in the daylight take flight.
In every quiet corner they reside,
Embers of insight, too bright to hide.

Standards and morals, a compass within,
The soul's silent guide amidst life's din.
Beliefs like stars, unseen in day's glare,
By night revealed, their guidance is fair.

Rising on pillars of unwavering thought,
A structure of convictions hard fought.
Each stone a testament of inner might,
In the fortress of faith, hearts take flight.

Rhythms of the Recluse

In the recluse's heart, rhythms resonate,
Beats of solitude for some, a dire fate.
Yet in the silence, a melody pure,
Sings of a peace most find in the obscure.

Hours unfold in a slow, steady cadence,
Each tick a note in the hermit's dance.
In the absence of clamor, thoughts align,
Finding in quietude, a rhythm divine.

Life's cacophony fades far away,
As a solitary soul finds its sway.
Its dance is measured, patient, and wise,
Each step a testament to the quiet it defies.

In the echo of a world left behind,
The recluse's heartbeats are intertwined.
With a symphony of serenity's creation,
A rhythm cherished, in silent elation.

Unvoiced Yearnings

In the stillness of a heart closed tight,
Lie unvoiced yearnings that shun the light.
Dreams unspoken, desires untold,
Passions that simmer, never to unfold.

Like whispers of a love never confessed,
Silent pangs in a lonely chest.
Yearnings that flutter, then fade to sleep,
In the depths of a soul, so private, so deep.

In every sigh, a wish concealed,
In each gaze, a hope unrevealed.
Longings linger in the quiet space,
A dance of shadows, an invisible chase.

Unvoiced yearnings, a silent plea,
For something more, to break free.
Yet in the caverns where they hide,
Lies a truth that cannot be denied.

Sketches of Serenity

In gentle strokes, the calm is drawn,
Early light of the unworried dawn.
An artist's hands sketch scenes of peace,
Where all the tumult comes to cease.

Across the canvas, hues blend and flow,
In quietude's arms, we watch time slow.
Moments captured in the softest light,
Portraits of tranquility, an exquisite sight.

Each brushstroke reveals a silent grace,
A tranquil place for the mind to embrace.
Where thoughts drift like leaves on a stream,
Sketches of serenity, a dreamer's dream.

In visions crafted from stillness' lore,
The heart finds a shore to quietly adore.
A masterpiece of the calmest spree,
The art of peace, a soul's sanctuary.

Veiled Verses

Beneath a shroud of twilight haze,
Upon the heart does mystery graze,
Words dance in elusive guise,
Hiding truths before our eyes.

Cloaked thoughts in shadowed vellum,
Scripted in a silent sanctum,
In each line, a secret dwells,
In each pause, a silence tells.

Whispers stir behind the veil,
Tales of love and loss regale,
Verses veiled capture the night,
Only to be freed by morning light.

Entwined with the ephemeral dream,
Poets weave the unseen seam,
Silent songs of heart and mind,
In veiled verses, we seek and find.

Embers of Memory

Glowing coals of yesteryears,
Warm the heart with past joys and fears,
Each ember, a moment caught in time,
A memory's dance, a life's chime.

They flicker under twilight's breath,
Shifting 'neath the ashes of death,
Glimmering in the mind's deep caves,
Illuminating forgotten graves.

With each recall, they spark to life,
Kindling laughter, rekindling strife,
A beacon through the veil of night,
Guiding us with their gentle light.

In the stillness of the quiet mind,
Embers of memory we find,
A fire that burns through sorrow and glee,
In their warmth, we let ourselves be.

Midnight Musings

In the depth of night's embrace,
Stars whisper tales through silent space,
Moonbeams pen the shadows' flight,
Scribing musings of the night.

A hush descends, the world at rest,
While thoughts untangle, neatly pressed,
Midnight's quilt, a dark expanse,
Under which contemplations dance.

The mind roams where daylight hides,
Across vast seas and mountainsides,
Traversing lands of dream and thought,
In the quietude, solace sought.

These midnight musings, soft and profound,
In the waning hours, wisdom is found,
The night's serene, enigmatic tune,
Is but a prelude to the dawn's monsoon.

Inner Universe Unfolding

A cosmos within, complex and deep,
Unfurling its secrets, it does not sleep,
Galaxies of thought spiral around,
In the silence, they're profound.

Nebulae of emotions swirl and blend,
A tapestry of being without end,
Within each pulse, life resonates,
Through each breath, the soul navigates.

Planets of memories orbit the mind,
Oft colliding, oft aligned,
A celestial dance of the inner scope,
Where hope orbits the star of hope.

In the unfolding universe inside,
The quiet truths we often hide,
Bloom into worlds yet to be explored,
In the heart's vastness, life is stored.

Serenades of the Inner Storm

In my heart, a tempest brews,
A silent song, a storm perused.
Wild winds wail, yet unheard,
Within, the echoes are inferred.

Emotions swirl like leaves in flight,
Each one struggles, battles, fights.
The lightning's strike, a wordless claim,
A heart's unrest, with no one to blame.

Thunderous thoughts, an internal roar,
The rhythm chaotic, an inner war.
Serenades lost in the howling gale,
A soul's refrain, a private tale.

Yet within the storm, a peace is known,
For in the chaos, seeds are sown.
Growth emerges from the strife,
Serenades of the storm, the song of life.

Ballads Behind Closed Doors

Behind closed doors, the ballads play,
Softly sung where memories stay.
Each note a whisper from the past,
A harmony meant to last.

The walls, they resonate with tales,
Of love and loss, where time avails.
The silent songs in shadows hide,
Ballads of hearts, side by side.

Eyes closed, the verses we can feel,
Each line, each chorus seems so real.
Quietly, the melodies implore,
Inviting us to dance once more.

Muffled tones to the outer ear,
Yet inside, play sonnets clear.
Ballads known to souls alone,
Behind closed doors, where love is sewn.

The Soul's Whispered Yearnings

In gentle whispers, dreams ascend,
A silent prayer, the heart doth send.
The soul speaks low of deeper things,
Of flight without the need for wings.

Yearnings rise like morning mist,
A teasing touch, a soft, sweet kiss.
Desires spoken without a sound,
In whispers deep, where truth is found.
The murmurs soft, the secret sighs,
The hidden hopes, the silent cries.
A soul's yearning, tender, hushed,
A quiet longing, in twilight brushed.

The night listens to these soft pleas,
As whispers float on the gentle breeze.
A soul's yearning, a wish conveyed,
In the silent sanctuary of night's shade.

Private Dances with Words

With words, I waltz in solitude,
A private dance, my thoughts pursued.
Letters twirl, they dip and sway,
In the mind's ballroom where they play.

Syncopated rhythm of the muse,
Each syllable, a step I choose.
In quietude, my pen does trace,
The intimate dance of written grace.

Expressions pirouette on the page,
A silent ballet for a personal stage.
In my retreat, where none can see,
Words and I dance, wild and free.

In solitude, the verse takes form,
A whispered waltz amid the storm.
Each word, a partner in the dance,
Private musings given a chance.

Musings Under the Moonlit Quill

Beneath the glow, the silver quill soars,
Over parchment, it dances and roars.
Illuming thoughts that night conceals,
In a dance of shadows, silence heals.

Strokes of moonlight, soft and gentle,
Crafting tales, sweet and sentimental.
Each word a footprint in timeless sands,
A narrative held in steady hands.

Verses pour like lunar tide,
Secrets in fluent script confide.
The quill, a key to locked away dreams,
Where reality is not as it seems.

In the quiet, under starry frills,
Whispers wake the moonlit quills.
Scripts of life, a nocturnal sigh,
Transcribing the language of the sky.

Pages Drenched in Thought

Each droplet a word, soaked with insight,
Pages laden with the echoes of plight.
Thoughts cascading like a relentless rain,
Inscribed with joy, embellished with pain.

The parchment, a sea of whirling emotion,
Waves of concepts, a deep, boundless ocean.
Every line a current, every curve a crest,
In the depths of ink, our truths come to rest.

Words whispered softly, in a fervent stream,
Narratives forged from a subconscious dream.
Pages drenched, each sentence a dove,
Spreading wings on notions of love.

Through the veil of each soaked phrase,
Visions clear like the morning's haze.
In thoughts submerged, our spirits dive,
And in these soggy pages, our minds revive.

Unspoken Words Between Lines

In the breaths between the ink,
Secrets hide and let us think.
Silent tales that shy away,
Just beyond what words convey.

In the quiet, letters bide,
Whispered conversations slide.
A tender script that's never heard,
The space between each written word.

Unvoiced sentiments reveal,
Only what the heart can feel.
Mute confessions, soft and lean,
In the margins, they convene.

Truth that's etched but never spoken,
Bonds that form but never broken.
Through the unsaid, we align,
Connecting dots between each line.

Secrets Inked in Shadows

Hushed are the strokes that the nightfall shrouds,
In the silence, the ink writes clouds.
Secrets hover, a veiled mist,
Stories cloaked in a twilight tryst.

Each letter carves out an arcane trail,
In the depths of dusk, truths prevail.
Words splay like a shadow's dance,
Mystery lined in every glance.

Tales inked in the dim, latent light,
Concealing their essences from sight.
Intimate whispers of the quill,
A clandestine world that night does fill.

Submerged in darkness, the secrets blend,
Where the echo of the heart won't end.
In the contours of the darkened sheath,
Lie the words that shadows breathe.

Silent Sighs of the Soul

Beneath the quiet twilight's glow,
A whisper travels soft and low,
Within the heart where none may see,
The silent sighs begin to flow.

Through the stillness of the night,
Each breath a shadow, out of sight,
The soul's unheard laments arise,
In the embrace of clandestine light.

A murmur trapped in endless time,
A dance of thoughts that softly chime,
The heartstrings play a silent tune,
In solitude, their echo climbs.

The world unaware remains,
As in the soul, the silence reigns,
Yet, in each sigh, the truth resides,
The soul's soft song is not in vain.

Undressed Emotions

Our masks fall to the ground, undone,
Veiling no more; the charade ends,
Bare feelings glisten 'neath the sun,
Undressed emotions now ascend.

Without pretense, they stand exposed,
In naked truth, they find their strength,
Revealing fears once tightly closed,
Tears wash away, at length.

Each heartbeat echoes raw and true,
A symphony of inner strife,
With every pulse, emotions brew,
The essence of our hidden life.

Discarding every shield and guise,
We let our deepest selves arise,
In vulnerability's eyes, we infer,
The beauty of our honest cries.

Lingering Touch of Words

Words, like fingers, trace the mind,
Leaving trails of thought behind,
Gentle whispers in the air,
A lingering touch that hearts ensnare.

Lines that carve through stone and time,
In lilting verse and hearty rhyme,
They speak of love, of dreams, of fears,
A touch that stays through passing years.

Echoes of a bygone day,
In memories, they twine and sway,
Caressing souls with vanished hands,
Their imprints stretch across life's sands.

So, let the words your spirit catch,
In their embrace, meanings attach,
With every line, a tender brush,
A lasting bond, in silence, hush.

Introspective Vows

In the quiet depths of thought,
Where battles fierce are inward fought,
Reflection's mirror, sharp and clear,
Shows the truths we hold so dear.

Promises to self we make,
Vows that sleep but never break,
In the soul's secluded bowers,
Lie these whispered, sacred powers.

To thine own self, always true,
In secret pledges, softly hew,
A fortitude that time endows,
In silent words, introspective vows.

As we navigate life's crowded maze,
Beneath the gaze of the public's daze,
It's the inner oath that we avow,
To keep us true to the here and now.

Pulse of Inner Musings

In the silent chamber of thoughts untold,
A rhythm of self, in whispers unfold.
Echoes of dreams that flutter and dance,
A quivering pulse, left to chance.

Lingering feelings in the soul's recess,
Glimmering hopes that softly impress.
Murmurs of wishes, secret desires,
Coursing within like silent fires.

Swayed by the tides of emotional seas,
Rippled reflections of life's decrees.
Beating in sync with time's tender rhymes,
A heart's silent musings, lost in chimes.

Embers of an Inner Flame

In the hearth of my spirit burns a quiet glow,
A fire fed on dreams that only I know.
Smoldering softly, an ember's embrace,
A warm, steady presence filling my space.

Crackling voices of vigor and might,
Flaring in darkness, creating light.
A dance of aspirations, bright and keen,
Projected in shadows only I have seen.

The blaze of passion, the spark of art,
Aflame with the essence of my heart.
They flicker and falter, yet still they claim,
The eternal vigil of an inner flame.

Whimsical Writings in the Dark

In the realm of midnight's ink-stained hue,
Dwell stories told and fictions new.
Scratching of quill on paper sable,
A nocturne's narrative, a moonlit fable.

Figments spun from the gossamer night,
A canticle spun in the absence of light.
Wanderings free, where thoughts embark,
Upon a parchment sky, a whimsical arc.

Verse woven from the loom of the mind,
Where fantasies roam and muses are kind.
In the quietude where visions embark,
Lie whimsical writings written in the dark.

Desires Wrapped in Parchment

Words traced with longing upon the sheet,
An epistle of the heart's rhythmic beat.
Wishes and dreams bundled tight,
In parchment clutches, away from sight.

A scroll of yearnings pulled by the seam,
Unfurling desires, a whispered dream.
Inked in silence, a quiet plea,
Sealed with wax, a fervent decree.

Each stroke a testament to silent prayer,
A chronicle of hope in written air.
Longings scribed with feathered quill,
Desires wrapped, but living still.

Sonnets Scribed in Secrecy

In twilight's hush, my pen begins to dance,
Upon the parchment, secrets twine and weave.
In every measured mark, a clandestine stance,
In every line, a heart's concealed reprieve.

Through silent hours, these whispered words are born,
A gentle cadence flowing, pure and deep.
They tell of love and longing, joy and mourn,
In inky veils where silent yearnings seep.

Serenade the stars with soft-spoken verse,
Adrift in dreams, these silent sonnets lie.
Each stanza holds a universe, diverse,
Each phrase, a secret 'neath the moonlit sky.

Tender Verses, Tender Truths

With tender verses writ upon my soul,
I weave the truths that tremble unexpressed.
In every word, emotion plays a role,
In every line, my inner thoughts confessed.

The whispers of a heart too scared to speak,
Find refuge in the rhythm of the rhyme.
In poetry, the strong made artfully weak,
In rhythm, reason paired with the sublime.

So tender are the truths that poets tell,
The soft-spun yarns that bind us through the years.
In every verse, a virtue's carousel,
In every word, the sum of all my fears.

Dusky Pages of Passion

Upon the dusky pages of my night,
I scribe the ardent pulses of my veins.
Each letter glowing with an inner light,
Each metaphor, the passion that remains.

Beneath a cloak of fading twilight's blush,
My quill ignites the passions held at bay.
Through inky rivers, feelings surge and rush,
In every line, my soul's flamboyant play.

A passionate ballet in shadows deep,
The pages hold my heart's unbridled race.
Within the script, the fiery secrets keep,
A testament to love's enduring grace.

Hushed Odes to Myself

In quietude, I pen odes to my being,
Self-reflections whispered to the night.
Within each verse, a fragment of my seeing,
A hushed confession in the soft moonlight.

To face the muse that dwells within my core,
With honest words, a silent dialogue.
This introspection I cannot ignore,
A quiet anthem in life's monologue.

In self-embrace, these muted verses flow,
A tranquil stream of consciousness revealed.
My private odes, where only shadows go,
The quiet truths that to myself I yield.

Timid Truths

Whispers linger in the silent shade,
Where timid truths are softly laid.
In the hush of dawn, they shyly wait,
Brushing the earth in a feathery state.

Tender are the murmurs of the heart,
Reluctantly from lips they part.
Gently swaying like a fragile leaf,
In the quietude, they find relief.

Shadows hold their unspoken fears,
In the twilight glow, truth nears.
Descend too soft, too slight to hear,
Yet in their silence, they draw near.

Underneath the starry veil, unspoken,
Timid truths exist, a cherished token.
Tales that tremble on the edge of night,
In the tender folds of dimming light.

Reticent Reveries

In the garden of thought, reveries bloom,
Veiled in the mist, they subtly loom.
Faint-hearted dreams, cast in twilight,
Dancing quietly, just out of sight.

Silent wishes, in the alcoves hide,
Reticent, in shadows they confide.
Whispered hopes in the silent hour,
Withdrawn petals of a shrinking flower.

In the cradle of dusk, they softly sigh,
Elusive as the stars up high.
Wary fantasies, draped in doubt,
Beneath the moonlight, they wander about.

Hold these reveries in a gentle clasp,
As they quiver within grasp.
Eluding words, they cannot stay,
In the world of speech, they fade away.

Chronicles of the Chaste

Untouched tales, pristine and pure,
Unwritten sagas that endure.
Innocent whispers that softly confide,
Chronicles of the chaste, side by side.

Pages unturned, secrets unspilled,
In the library of virtue, quietly thrilled.
Narratives noble, in their nature chaste,
Carved in the marble halls of taste.

Through the annals of time, they remain intact,
Their essence whole, their virtue exact.
Writings that breathe in candor's air,
Scripts that the dust of deceit spare.

Pure chronicles, told without a stain,
Echoing softly, a sacred refrain.
In the glow of honor, they stand amassed,
In the chronicles of the chaste, truth holds fast.

Secreted Sentiments

In the silent sanctum of the heart,
Where secreted sentiments impart.
Words veiled in the echoes of the mind,
Feelings that seek, but rarely find.

Buried deep, they rest concealed,
In the quiet corners, quietly sealed.
Unvoiced emotions of depth untold,
Guarded treasures that never grow old.

Muffled murmurs we scarce understand,
Like etchings of time on soft sand.
Undisclosed desires that inward bloom,
In solitude's garden, away from gloom.

Whispers locked in the silent vault,
Of love, of fear, of dreams that halt.
In the vaults of the soul, they lie latent,
Deep sentiments, secreted, patient.

Whispers to Myself

In the quiet of the night I speak,
The soft murmur of thoughts run deep.
Words tiptoe in my solitary glee,
Whispers to myself, a secret symphony.

Within the hush, my spirit soars,
In gentle echoes behind closed doors.
Talking to shadows that hug the walls,
My inner voice, a friend who calls.

Solace found in the mute discussions,
Untangling threads of life’s confusions.
Silent words, each a comforting balm,
My mind's refuge, a place of calm.

Whispers to myself, unspun so clear,\n nBare truths to heed, only I hear.
As daybreak comes, they retreat so shy,
In whispers to myself, I bid goodbye.

In Silent Verses

Beneath the tumult that roars loud and wild,
My thoughts compose in silent verses, mild.
Each word a petal in the wind's embrace,
In tender rhymes, my quiet solace.

Muted feelings that the heart doth weave,
Are the silent verses that the soul believes.
Distilled in quietude, away from daylight's bustle,
They flow and form in an unseen rustle.

In love and loss, in joy and sorrow's hearse,
The silent verses bear the universe.
Scribing on air, they leave no trace,
Transient beauties of a lonesome space.

Hush-hewed stanzas speak without a sound,
In silent verses where my truth is found.
Beneath life's clatter, they silently chant,
A closet poet's quietest, yet firmest, rant.

Echoes of a Hidden Heart

Echoes of my heart, veiled out of sight,
A murmur beneath the cacophony of light.
Resonating softly, a discreet riff,
A hidden heart's call, ephemeral as a whiff.

Through corridors of my introspect,
The silent beat in its crypt reflects.
A dappled past to the fore it brings,
In echoes, my inner sanctum sings.

Veiled emotions in gentle repartee,
Ricochet lightly in silent spree.
Each a testament to what's held dear,
Echoes of the heart, only I can hear.

At night they rise, then coyly part,
A silent sonnet from a hidden heart.
Their timbre wrapped in the cloak of night,
The echoes within, my beacon light.

Confessions at Midnight

When spirits of night softly creep,
And daylight's din is put to sleep,
Time to lay bare my whispered confiteor,
To confess at midnight, my heart's outpour.

In cloak of darkness, truths unfurl,
Tales of yesterdays in my mind whirl,
Spoken only to Luna and her stars so bright,
Are confessions whispered to the still of night.

Untold secrets find their voice at last,
The veils of day's pretense are cast,
In the quietude, my soul's candid script,
Where confessions at midnight are safely kept.

To the listening silence, I bare my mind,
As the clock chimes, my fears unwind.
The night nonjudgmental, receiving my heart's plea,
In confessions at midnight, I set them free.

Fragile Rhymes

Upon the whisper of morning's light,
Through the silence of the coming night,
Words like glass cast upon the times,
Melodies broken, those fragile rhymes.

Echoes dance in hallowed halls,
Where shadows flicker and memory calls,
Each stanza, a delicacy unwinds,
In the grasp of delicate, fragile rhymes.

Tender verses, they fray and tear,
Like woven silk threads in disrepair,
Clinging to moments, slipping chimes,
Beauty held within those fragile rhymes.

And yet with each unsteady line,
The heart's deep truths they do refine,
In whispered verses, life reclines,
Preserved forever, fragile rhymes.

Unraveling Affection

In the hush of twilight's embrace,
Where shadows merge and hearts race,
Love's fabric starts to loosely lace,
Our unraveling affection’s face.

Thread by thread, it comes undone,
Under the fading, weary sun,
Once bright hues to monochrome transition,
In the quietude of love’s remission.

Still, in the unraveling, a beauty found,
As emotions spill, unbound,
Gentle whispers, without inflection,
Tell the tale of faded affection.

Within each strand, a story lies,
Of passion's flame, in smoldered cries,
Yet even as it wanes in all direction,
We cling to remnants, unraveling affection.

Undercurrents of the Mind

Beneath the calm exterior stream,
Lie undercurrents of a waking dream,
Subconscious murmurs, softly entwined,
In the shadowed depths of the mind.

Gentle ripples in the conscious sea,
Hide the depth of inner plea,
Whispers, secrets, of the confined,
Lurk in the undercurrents of the mind.

Swift and deep, the currents flow,
Carrying thoughts we barely know,
Hidden fears, to us they bind,
Caught in the undercurrents of the mind.

There, in the silence, truth can roar,
In the stillness, one can explore,
The mysteries that within us wind,
Revealing undercurrents of the mind.

Soul's Soliloquy

In the quiet hours of contemplation,
My soul speaks in silent oration,
Thoughts unspoken, forming slowly,
Voicing the lines of a soul's soliloquy.

Amidst life's incessant, noisy crowd,
Soulful whispers often go unbowed,
Yet in solitude, it speaks solely,
Translating life in a soul's soliloquy.

It tells of joys and of sorrows deep,
Of promises made and left to keep,
In verse it renders life's anthology,
Through every stanza of a soul's soliloquy.

For within its speech, both bold and shy,
Lies the essence of the how and why,
In that inner space where we are truly free,
The heart composes its soul's soliloquy.

Solitary Serenades

Beneath the moon's soft silvery glow,
Alone where whispering breezes blow,
A quiet song to the starlit sky,
Harmony blooming in the night so shy.

In the solitude, the heart does find,
Melodies that soothe the troubled mind,
Strains of peace ascend and fade,
In the nocturne of the lonely glade.

Strings of the soul quietly plead,
In every note, a hidden seed,
Planted in the silence of the dark,
A symphony composed by the nightingale's lark.

Unheard are the tunes that gently weep,
The secrets that the shadows keep,
Yet, in solitude their beauty sways,
In these solitary serenades.

Murmured Desires

In the hush of the dimming light,
Where dreams caress the edge of night,
Words unspoken, tender and rare,
Murmured desires in the cool evening air.

Whispered wishes in the quiet space,
Longing for a tender embrace,
Each uttered sigh, a secret confession,
Lost in the abyss of silent expression.

The flicker of candle, the shadows dance,
In the stillness, giving passion a chance,
Yearning for touch, a fervent fire,
A heart alight with muted desire.

So let the wind carry what lips dare not say,
Let the stars hear the pleas that we lay,
For in the murmur, love does not tire,
Within soft-spoken winds, lie murmured desires.

Echoes of Intimacy

Whispers in the chamber of the heart,
Echoes of intimacy, a tender art,
Two souls entwined in silent repartee,
In the depths where words are superfluous to say.

An indelible trace left with a glance,
Within a touch, the spirits dance,
In the closeness, a comforting decree,
A vow of presence, eternally to be.

Soft breaths exchanging life's warm creed,
An interlace of need and need,
In each echo, a promise to satisfy,
A covenant of closeness, that time can't deny.

So, listen close to the beating hearts' symphony,
Its rhythm binds beyond what eyes can see,
In love's resonance, we find unity,
Beneath the surface, live echoes of intimacy.

Hidden Chambers

Deep within the castle of the soul,
Lies hidden chambers, stories untold,
Walls lined with velvet memories sweet,
Sealed away from the world's unkind heat.

Each chamber a trove of secret dreams,
Where time flows in idyllic streams,
Cloaked in the hush of private thought,
A sanctuary from battles fought.

There in the quiet, the self does slumber,
Away from reality's plundering thunder,
Innermost sanctums locked with care,
Guarding the essences of who we are.

Seek not to know each veiled room,
For some are filled with light, others with gloom,
Sacrosanct havens from life's clamors,
The soul’s most dear, these hidden chambers.

Printed in the USA
CPSIA information can be obtained
at www.ICGtesting.com
LVHW081241021223
765302LV00010B/154

9 789916 394663